One Hundred Lockdown Sonnets

One Hundred Lockdown Sonnets

Jacqueline Saphra

Nine
Arches
Press

One Hundred Lockdown Sonnets
Jacqueline Saphra

ISBN: 978-1-913437-31-2

Copyright © Jacqueline Saphra, 2021.

Cover artwork and page illustrations © Sophie Herxheimer, 2021.
www.sophieherxheimer.com

All rights reserved. No part of this work may be reproduced, stored or transmitted in any form or by any means, graphic, electronic, recorded or mechanical, without the prior written permission of the publisher.

Jacqueline Saphra has asserted her right under Section 77 of the Copyright, Designs and Patents Act 1988 to be identified as the author of this work.

First published January 2021 by:

Nine Arches Press
Unit 14, Sir Frank Whittle Business Centre,
Great Central Way, Rugby.
CV21 3XH
United Kingdom
www.ninearchespress.com

Printed in the United Kingdom by Imprint Digital.

Nine Arches Press is supported using public funding by Arts Council England.

Supported using public funding by
ARTS COUNCIL ENGLAND

Jacqueline Saphra's *The Kitchen of Lovely Contraptions* (flipped eye, 2011) was shortlisted for the Aldeburgh First Collection Prize. *If I Lay on my Back I Saw Nothing but Naked Women* (The Emma Press, 2014) won the Saboteur Award for Best Collaborative Work. *All My Mad Mothers* (Nine Arches Press, 2017) was shortlisted for the T.S. Eliot prize. Two of her sonnet sequences *A Bargain with the Light: Poems after Lee Miller* (2017) and *Veritas: Poems After Artemisia* (2020) are published by Hercules Editions. Her third collection, *Dad, Remember You Are Dead* was published by Nine Arches Press in 2019. She is a founder member of Poets for the Planet, lives in London and teaches at The Poetry School.

Contents

Foreword		13
I	I'm standing at the starting line	15
II	*Are you fearful you might see*	16
III	Alas there is no plan	17
IV	the strange part of this wild new world	18
V	What can a poem do?	19
VI	The first week is nearly gone	20
VII	I've had a bad review	21
VIII	And suddenly it's love	22
IX	This could be hell or heaven	23
X	The days are falling down	24
XI	He enters through your mouth	25
XII	The lockdown's tight	26
XIII	Today, in search of hope	27
XIV	This evening her majesty	28
XV	I'm overcome by beauty	29
XVI	We love the NHS	30
XVII	A mist has settled on the Thames	31

XVIII	We gather round the plate	32
XIX	Here's bread, here's wine	33
XX	The men are digging trenches	34
XXI	Men are boxing	35
XXII	And back to rage again	36
XXIII	London's gone psychedelic	37
XXIV	Big news	38
XXV	The men with masks and mallets	39
XXVI	It seems that we forgot	40
XXVII	My day begins with green	41
XXVIII	The Moon's a virgin body	42
XXIX	aaagh you may be sick	43
XXX	Out of the cataclysm	44
XXXI	Rukshana	45
XXXII	The whole of London's going	46
XXXIII	The president has shamed you	47
XXXIV	The brokers love a long-stemmed rose	48
XXXV	Of course the strategy's a scam	49
XXXVI	Here at the entrance	50
XXXVII	Near-biped wanderer	51
XXXVIII	Any farm would welcome him	52
XXXIX	Come on	53

XL	Podcasts!	54
XLI	And suddenly it's fear	55
XLII	The Oracle of Omaha	56
XLIII	Today's revelation	57
XLIV	So dead is a real word	58
XLV	It's clickbait	59
XLVI	How can we change our lives	60
XLVII	I'd seen the bunting	61
XLVIII	Our home is its own universe	62
XLIX	*My honourable friends*	63
L	Death takes centre stage	64
LI	I often try to write	65
LII	I have learned	66
LIII	After a normal day of woe	67
LIV	Perception flips	68
LV	Who sends their children off to school?	69
LVI	I'm lost	70
LVII	This is a space	71
LVIII	The city green is colonised	72
LIX	Remember Brick Lane Sundays?	73
LX	Where did they find these	74
LXI	Should we or should we not?	75

LXII	The green is calling	76
LXIII	Downing Street does its best	77
LXIV	I'm nearly feeling sorry	78
LXV	Hydroxychloroquine	79
LXVI	suppose the flowers	80
LXVII	The nurse unfolds	81
LXVIII	George Floyd	82
LXIX	*Now, strike a pose*	83
LXX	*Everyone is sacred*	84
LXXI	The dress doesn't fit	85
LXXII	Imagine that the evil walks	86
LXXIII	It was early March	87
LXXIV	Yesterday was hope	88
LXXV	The Sad is feeling it today	89
LXXVI	Maddie's hit the headlines	90
LXVII	Johnson plays with thunder	91
LXVIII	It's like living underwater	92
LXIX	Today I tuned out	93
LXXX	I want my old life back	94
LXXXI	Slipped under the radar	95
LXXXII	In flux and disarray	96

LXXXIII	When all the grief is over	97
LXXXIV	The toss and heat	98
LXXXV	Runners create their own slipstream	99
LXXXVI	This year someone papped	100
LXXXVII	There are certain things	101
LXXXVIII	The anthropologists	102
LXXXIX	And suddenly it's tears	103
XC	The day was perfect	104
XCI	I dreamed all night of sonnets	105
XCII	It's Monday and the news is in	106
XCIII	Our papers tell us things	107
XCIV	My love	108
XCV	I can satirise it all I like	109
XCVI	Come on Spotify, not him again	110
XCVII	Today a not-so-cool surprise	111
XCVIII	Everyone cheats a little	112
XCVIX	Well, it's a job	113
C	My loves, this is my last	114

Acknowledgements and Thanks   116

Foreword

At the start of the first Lockdown, I started writing a journal, thinking that the discipline might be useful as a way of keeping a record of life at the time. It was one of the most tedious writing tasks I've ever undertaken and I knew instantly that I had to find another way: a poet's way. A daily sonnet seemed a challenge I might be able to meet and I knew from past experience that the technical aspects would give me structure and focus. This maddening process of giving shape to the unshapeable paradoxically kept me sane, giving me a boundaried form to chart my own internal journey as well as external events.

There was no projected end to this venture, but I had never imagined I'd be able or willing to keep going for one hundred days of many challenges, mostly not poetic ones. But alleluia, the sonnet saved me! 'Eternal glory to the inventor of the sonnet', declared Paul Valéry, to which I can only say 'Amen'.

Jacqueline Saphra,
10th January 2021, London, Lockdown 3

Sonnet I   23rd March 2020

'PM "Stay at home. This is a national emergency"' – The Guardian

I'm standing at the starting line. Am I allowed
to share my shadows if I disinfect?
How do I dodge the shedders in the crowd,
the howls of strangers? Watch me attempt
the daily joy of blossoms, pink of hope
before they fall, ditch the questions, wait,
inhale the spring, ascend the hopeful slope
to summer; then wander home to isolate.
O small, unwholesome sofa, keep me safe,
don't make me scroll again for risk and grief.
Instead I'll do the work, try to be brave,
return to what I love; pen-scratch of faith.
I'll let the sonnet school me like a child
learning the language, open and purified.

Sonnet II   24th March 2020

'*1.3bn population of India are placed on lockdown*' – BBC News

Are you fearful you might see a lot
of corpses in the Thames? my uncle says
on FaceTime from New Jersey. *No I'm not,*
I answer, *get a grip. It's early days.*
But he's off, a doctor pessimist
who's seen his share of death and knows the ropes:
Remember Spanish flu, Ebola, plague pits?
The data speaks; don't be a slave to hope,
think of Iran: the waiting graves so vast
they've caught the images on satellite.
The signal's faint, the water flows too fast,
the tide is turning, do I hear him right?
My old life slips its knot, sails into the sun,
rounds the riverbend and *poof!* it's gone.

Sonnet III   25th March 2020

'Trump says the US is beginning to see
"the light at the end of the tunnel"' – BBC News

Alas there is no plan, there are no eggs,
no bread, compassion's nearly out of stock,
but we can walk together in the park
keeping our distance. Spring is here; she bends
her spine towards the light and takes her place
amid the joy of things. She will not stop
her rhymes of blossoms reaching out and up
towards the sun, she will not slow her pace
towards full-frontal ecstasy, she knows
only one way to hold this world. Our pain
is not her pain. We must move on, stay close
without touching, share the climbing light of day,
build our wall of faith against the flood
and try to talk of other things. Like love.

Sonnet IV   26th March 2020

'UK *death toll reaches 465*' – The Guardian

the strange part of this wild new world is what
you do not do you do not check the date
you do not know the time or moan a lot
you do not change your clothes or punctuate
you do not rush to catch the daily train
you do not grab a healthy snack at Prêt
you do not push the biscuit tin away
you do not fast or fuss about your weight
you do not brush your hair you do not say
you are too busy for a chat you do not keep
a diary you do not mortify
your flesh at double pump you do not weep
so easily for once you dare not think
your pain is somehow different or unique

Sonnet V   27th March 2020

'Global cases pass 500,000. Health Secretary and Prime Minister test positive for coronavirus' – BBC News

What can a poem do? What use are words?
The glassy river barely speaks today,
undisturbed by human vessels, left to the birds.
Even the muse has nothing left to say.
O, winged and wayward creature: open, shut
by turns, depending on the weight of air,
the dredge of dreams, the long lurch of the heart,
I need your song to tell me where you are.
Give me a lift! Throw me a line! Let me out!
I swear I'll keep my distance from the others,
grim and grounded in the library of doubt.
Find me in the stacks among the feathers
searching for a cure where there is none,
pacing the white shelves of my lexicon.

Sonnet VI   28th March 2020

'UK *death toll reaches 1000*'

The first week is nearly gone. I stay in bed
tight-folded into dream and hold
my one-tale tongue, dozing away from dread.
Sleep, old lover, has never been so bold
nor so attentive: promises of peace
and flowers, clever tricks with camomile
to close a mind that's longing for release.
I'll wake you when it's over. Rest a while.
I'm half-seduced, curled up inside my nest
of fears. But wait! Don't I love to be alive?
The morning calls, small joys are manifest;
the coffee croons, the brimming day's arrived,
the kids are singing harmonies. I'm up
for this: I risk and rise and fill my cup.

Sonnet VII   29th March 2020

'Outbreak will get worse before it gets better PM tells nation' – The Guardian

I've had a bad review. I can't believe
I care. Oh what? Still this flush of shame,
familiar, meaningless, with griefs
far greater waiting as a perfect pain
roars towards us like a tidal wave.
There's comfort in these old indulgences;
why feel the real when I can touch the page
and angst over artistic transience?
It's spring. There's sleet. I'll take a freezing walk
with my denial, curse the critics,
enjoy the forward winding of the clocks,
pander to my existential crisis,
spurn the mortal curve, pick up my pen
and write this sonnet as the wave descends.

Sonnet VIII   30th March 2020

'... a croaky-sounding Boris Johnson said ... his Conservative predecessor Margaret Thatcher was wrong when she famously declared "there is no such thing as society"' – BBC News

And suddenly it's love no matter who
I'm writing to. It used to be *warm wishes,*
kind regards or *yours sincerely*. Now
it's *lots of love* to all with rows of kisses.
What's going on? I only have to watch the news
to find I'm helplessly adoring half the world.
O holy humankind, I'm weak with gratitude.
I'm loose like laundry off the line and if I could
I'd hug the postman and the street sweeper,
I'd weep into the stiff neck of the woman
at the checkout, I'd smooch the doctor
and the nurse before I knew what I was doing.
O flamboyant faith, O trusting soul,
I am prostrate before you; keep me whole.

Sonnet IX   31ˢᵗ March 2020

'FTSE 100 suffers worst quarter since 1987' – BBC News

'From Quartz massages to giant floating ice baths, here are the top wellness destinations for 2020' – Canary Wharf Magazine, March 2020

This could be hell or heaven. Who knows which?
We roam your concourses, we marvel at
your rooftop gardens and your ghoulish kitsch,
your restaurants and bars, your glitzy tat,
your automatic escalators still
climbing to nowhere. Where are your men in suits,
your quickstep waiters, gyms and spin-class thrills,
your oatmilk lattés and your champagne flutes,
your breathless trains, your pits and palaces?
We stroll amid this air of nothing, blow
our cash on faked-up meals on empty terraces
as dust settles on your public pianos
and your temples, vermin do their doings
and rats claim their rightful place among the ruins.

Sonnet X   1st April 2020

"This is going to be a very painful, very, very painful two weeks" – Donald Trump
'The outbreak is the biggest global challenge since World War Two' – BBC News.

The days are falling down and falling out,
they have no discipline. They are at ease,
on furlough, otherwise engaged, they flout
the rules, they don't respect our boundaries.
The hours are down the pub, far gone, they shock
and riot at the remnants of our lives,
they mock our forward plans, they kick the clock,
they scorn our coffee dates, our cocktail nights,
our *must not miss,* our meetings with the boss.
We rise at noon, we eat at three, as time
runs on unchecked, unquantified and lost.
We sweep our calendars only to find
parades of dust; our baffled futures track
the voided pages of our almanacs.

Sonnet XI 2nd April 2020

'*Confirmed global cases pass a million*' – BBC News

He enters through your mouth, plays on your tongue,
but we don't know it yet. He heaves his weight
into your throat, descends into your lungs,
he listens for your breathing, celebrates
his smartness, chants his doom-filled runes
and mutters curses at your talk of trips
and futures. He spits his filthy tunes
into your salad bowl; he slurps and licks
your cups and plates. Assassin tipped
for victory, he drowns you out, he won't permit
your cultured lamentations. *Who gives a shit
about your life*! he shrieks, and soon you're sick.
Now you cough and cough; I give you all my love
laced with white pills – it may not be enough.

Sonnet XII   3rd April 2020

Beijing 'aims to turn national disaster into global triumph' – The Guardian

The lockdown's tight, the walls are thin; my son
is teaching English on the internet
to Chinese kids, a half-heard conversation.
Can you juggle, Monica? Fix this carrot.
When will you take flight, Clarence? Lend me your home.
Angel, do you know birds, the blessed heights,
the floating feather? Angel! Your back has grown
a pair of silken wings to hold the light.

Angel haunts me: one small girl, arms outstretched
on her perch high above a distant street.
But who will catch her, poised at the edge
of a common language as she leaps
into the future? Me? I put my dread on pause,
I fix it. Angel rises through the mist and soars.

Sonnet XIII   4th April 2020

'Fears for lockdown over weekend of sunshine' – BBC News

Today, in search of hope, air and solace
I walked down Cable Street. *Hello history,*
I said, *hello fascists, hello moral compass,*
hello barricades. But no-one heard me speak.
The boys were on the laughing gas, the shops
were selling fags and beer, a runner spat,
a cyclist nearly ran me down, I dropped
my optimism, made some notes, turned back.
Now as I write and news leaks through
the wall, the enemy is hard to spot.
Remember East End women at their windows
emptying their bins and chamber pots
on Blackshirts; a time when right was right and wrong
was wrong and evil wore a uniform.

Sonnet XIV   5th April 2020

'Queen took HUGE *health risk to film tonight's coronavirus speech*' – Daily Express

This evening her majesty will share
her royal life hacks. Huzzah! *Stay at home,*
eschew the public parks, comb your own hair,
don't overfeed the corgis, let the nanny go,
abjure the banquets and the balls, don't shake
the hands of other toothless servants of
the state and do not keep yourself awake
fretting for the butler. Show some resolve!
If we could we'd open up the royal purse –
but think of British pride. Do what we do!
Why give your billions to the NHS?
Clap the carers! Light your castle blue!
Be thrifty! Sack some staff, self-isolate
and ground 'The Royal Flight'. Make Britain great!

Sonnet XV 6th April 2020

'Too early to consider lockdown exit strategy'– Dominic Raab

I'm overcome by beauty – god, these blossoms
conjured from the air! Where did they come from,
sudden spheres of pink and jostle, fistfuls
of primal love, so transient, so common.
Who said *This too shall pass*? Like everyone
I'm looking for the signs. Am I naïve
to trust these startled gifts of April sun?
Despite my alternating panic and relief,
addiction to the fix of internet,
the lull of Netflix nights and doldrum days,
my dooms and zooms, my failed attempts
at sourdough starters, virtual party games,
I love this life, this life I made: I wake
in praise, I bring the light, I do not break.

Sonnet XVI   7th April 2020

'...the government's chief scientific adviser Sir Patrick Vallance told Tuesday's Downing Street briefing 'the number of coronavirus cases in the UK could be moving in the right direction'

'Boris Johnson is a fighter and will recover' — Dominic Raab

We love the NHS: while this useless case lies
in hospital, some flunkey bangs the drum
of British triumph, blagging it. Dumb
and closeted, no breath left to agonise,
the sick man leaves his friends to fraternise
with fools. With all their superpowers gone
they faff and fidget, hack and hum
predicting pomp and froth and better times.
They conjure flattened curves and stocks of masks,
they play the numbers while sleepless nurses cry
at ends of shifts filming selfies in their cars,
the people sweat, the ventilators sigh,
the doctors go about their tragic tasks,
the curve ascends, death crowds the corridors.

Sonnet XVII 8th April 2020

'This City now doth, like a garment, wear
The beauty of the morning' – William Wordsworth

'They tell us coronavirus is a great leveller. It's not. It's much
much harder if you're poor' – Emily Maitlis, BBC Newsnight

A mist has settled on the Thames, the air
is clearer than it's been for years. Inhale.
Who knew that breath could be so beautiful?
The stillness rings like something pure,
a gown of water shimmers on the shore,
I pause to hold this heaven; then the pull
of change upstream: tuneless bell
of piling rigs, the underbelly of the river
laid open, her hidden darknesses given
to the poetry of super-sewer,
unromantic, necessary; human waste
and wastage managed by maskless men
taking their chances for a living wage,
the unsung heroes of our sunken age.

Sonnet XVIII 9th April 2020

'This Passover, the seder is virtual. The plague is real' – CNN

'The Jewish Chronicle and Jewish news to go into liquidation' – BBC News

We gather round the plate, its song of songs,
the history of birds on lilt and loop
of leaf and bloom, a blue of painted spring
to celebrate millennia of hope
against erasure. Did I say *we gather*?
Each in our little space, we make a grid
of faces. I feel I've loved you all forever.
For now, this is the closest we can get.
We work our shaky melody, we bear the weight
of memory and just for now, we're not alone.
The plagues are everywhere. We tell it straight,
we truly know it now. We fill our lungs,
inhale some joy, exhale a kind of unison,
singing with blue birds on a china plate.

Sonnet XIX   10th April 2020

'Boris Johnson almost took one for the team' – Stanley Johnson

Here's bread, here's wine that tastes of passion fruit
and freedom. Let us drink, our little doors
thrown open to the river. The tides are good,
we have each other now, we lucky four.
I hold my luck against my chest; I trust
this love as if it were an amulet.
I nurse my faith, I am an idiot.
Luck is fickle, luck is not built to last,
but luck is all we have and we are blessed.
We're getting used to this. We sip the wine,
we soap our hands, we count the deaths,
we stress and squabble in our little nest
of love and pain. We try to save the time
and make the most of this. We do our best.

Sonnet XX   11th April 2020

'New York City officials have hired contract laborers to bury the dead in its potter's field on Hart Island' – Reuters

The men are digging trenches. The drones
are on the move, filming, marking the day:
new graves to hold the homeless bones
of the diseased, unloved, unknown, unclaimed.
The dead are wrapped in body bags, then placed
inside the coffins, names scrawled on the lids.
The men-for-hire stack up the bodies, laid
in rows three deep. Earth will cover this
the way she always has. The plague has come
again; the mother of us all cradles her dead
and weeps. We cannot feel it. Rapt in the hum
of drones, we hover, doubting, overhead.
Surely that toytown island can't be real:
its men in yellow, black earth, charnel fields.

Sonnet XXI   12th April 2020

'Sombre day as death toll exceeds 10,000' – BBC News

Men are boxing on the morning lawns,
parks are rife with women bold in lycra
sweating under blossom at their squat
and lunge, and everyone is running, though
there is nowhere to run. It's much too hot
outside but then it's hot as hell at home –
for now, now is the season of the meltdown;
cabin fever, daily heats of fear.
Dare I speak of rage, or do I go too far?
It flares at will, it rises at the news,
it sets our hopes aflame, a saboteur,
casual like a vandal with nothing to lose,
it roams deserted streets with trace and track,
it finds us ready; we don't hold it back.

Sonnet XXII 13th April 2020

'*Home Secretary Priti Patel insists there is support available for at-risk women as charities report massive increase in calls*' – The Guardian

And back to rage again; distilled, confined,
it finds new entrances. Somewhere, a woman
shakes between four walls, her days unwind
like rope, love's noose, as daily bulletins
parade their numbers, not her numbers. Twisted,
silent, somewhere in a hothouse room,
a man is letting go, finding his fists.
The social offers: *hashtag you are not alone,*
the cops are out on call, sirens streak the night
with platitudes: *be safe, go home, stay home.*
But home is gormless, earless, voiceless, blind,
it lets the blood rush in, it lets the curse run on
and beyond mercy, behind some frozen door
a man parades his shame, another woman falls.

Sonnet XXIII   14th April 2020

'Yes, I think you can say the worst is over' – Governor Andrew Cuomo

London's gone psychedelic: parakeets
glow luminous through branches, the high grass
is surely tripping with the trees on speed.
The sky is flirty blue, the clouds are cast
in platinum, leaf speaks in tongues
of awe as fledgling redbreasts get their kicks
on Stepney Green, crowd-sourcing their songs.
Nature performs her usual tricks: pulling chicks
from eggs and rabbits out of rabbits. *Voila!* –
and today I'm walking out with Dolly Parton
Nine to Five, glutted with song and colour,
sun turned to extra shine, my heart on
double shifts. A shaking happiness steals in.
It will not last; I hold it while I can.

Sonnet XXIV 15th April 2020

'*Hospitals and care homes to allow goodbyes to dying*' – BBC News

'*Watchdog bans ads for Burger King 'vegan-suitable' Rebel*' – The Guardian

Big news: our trust has been misplaced:
even the *Rebel Whopper* isn't what it claims.
Misrepresented as the blameless face
of flesh, it consorts with mayonnaise,
it reeks of filth and abattoirs in dreams
of tallow, travesty of patty in a bun.
Once we thought there was a plan; now it seems
truth falls away, old certainties are gone.
The killers are at work: whom do they kill
safe behind their autocues? They hone
their lies of herd and stun, they fire at will
and leave us helpless in our pens to moan
and ruminate, to live inside the dread
of human solitude and mourn our dead.

Sonnet XXV   16th April 2020

'UK Lockdown extended for at least three weeks'

The men with masks and mallets have destroyed
a small world on the floor above. I heard
the debris crashing through the ceiling void
while I was writing this, looking for words.
I felt the whole house shake. The weirded day
was sinking fast. Squinting through clouds of black
to find this poem, I had nothing left to say.
Yeah, poetry. Ha ha! What use is that?
The sky is falling! All I do is howl
and hawk inside this hopeless shell of doom.
Where is the luminous and loveable?
The dust has dulled the lustre of this room
and I, the lightweight drinker, fold at last:
startle of whisky, ice and crystal glass.

Sonnet XXVI   17th April 2020

'Ministers back 21 more research projects to fight COVID 19'

It seems that we forgot the Easter hunt
again. Our days dissolve, our hours collapse,
the minutes melt and shift, they cut and run,
they change their shape like sub-atomic rats
who eat their daily weight in time and space.
We're bright enough; why can't we use our heads?
Why can't we put the season in its place?
It's not as if we haven't got the eggs,
but what's the point? Who cares? The chocolate chicks
are melting fast and we don't have the time
to lift the risky lids and check the box
for vermin; the rats are only in our minds,
surely. The long days screech, the nights are rough.
We lie awake and flinch at every cough.

Sonnet XXVII   18th April 2020

'Boris bounces back to get Britain moving' – Daily Mail

My day begins with green, like tea or grass,
I'm learning Cantonese and Mandarin,
I'm reading *Ulysses* and *Gormenghast*
and Plato while I'm training to be thin.
I'm shedding all my doubts, I'm knitting sieves
and sand, I write a symphony a week.
I grow my own arugula, I live
on air, philosophy and ancient Greek.
I'm breeding ants and sheep and minotaurs
to save my mental health. I do not want
for company or mutton, wool or horn.
The PhD is done, I'm looking hot,
James Joyce has said my novel's bloody great
and Mervyn Peake has asked me on a date.

Sonnet XXVIII   19ᵗʰ April 2020

'The US president recently signed an executive order stating America
has the right to explore and use resources from outer space' – BBC news

The moon's a virgin body, open to
the drill. Dig her down to the bone,
pools of moon-blood gushing through
your pipes and pumps, let lithium
and cobalt fall into your great machines.
Bring on the rocket men; it's time to scratch
the lunar itch, to occupy the dream,
to lunge into the void and vacuum, smash
the natives, bring victory from the colonies
in plundered riches, interstellar thrills.
History says *Pick a virus, any virus;*
clean up with covid, typhus, syphilis.
The poor and weak remain expendable;
nobody will remember those you kill.

Sonnet XXIX   20th April 2020

'Coronavirus: 'Low confidence' over arrival of PPE from Turkey' – BBC News

aaargh you may be sick it's hard to tell
you're working out and aaargh you're fighting fit
and aaargh your doom is entering the ring the bell
goes ding another round of panic aaargh don't quit
keep on your toes and aaargh it's Death to win
he holds his corner aaargh he's had his botox done
the devil bless his blowfly fist and sickle grin
and aaargh his crimson kiss is smack and stun
he throws a punch and aaargh you're down you suck
some ice you try to run and aaargh what luck
the nurse arrives she's got her binbag on
she goes ungloved the ventilator's stuck
her rusty needle's picking at your lungs
you hear her, maskless, weeping in the dark

Sonnet XXX   21st April 2020

'Eastern Europeans to be flown in to pick fruit and veg'

Out of the cataclysm something sweet
has dropped like orchard fruit dislodged by wind;
through stew and bruise, it sugars at your feet
humble with scent of rot. You cup your palms
and pick it up. Is it a poem? You touch the tip
of madness, squint through the blur of time; the clock
has lost her hands, dark juice oozes and drips.
Can you cure it? Life has run amock,
but what the hell Saphra? Why this crazy trip?
The orchard's full of windfalls, let them rot.
They're not for you. You need to get a grip.
Pack up, go home and drop the stupid fruit,
it doesn't need you. Let nature take its course;
it makes its own arrangements; you make yours.

Sonnet XXXI   22nd April 2020

'Coronavirus: Dominic Raab vows to hit 100k test target in eight days' – BBC News

'Boots the chemist: championing everyone's right to feel good'

Rukshana, I've been standing in this queue
for hours, but can't deny I have the time
to wait and watch the lucky ones pass through
the portals of your soothing sanctum.
Rukshana of the lovely name, I bless
your flat shoes, your kind gatekeeper grin,
please let me in Rukshana, ease my stress,
dispense the cure, bring on the medicine.
O hopeful hawker of the spell and charm,
lead me down the aisle; show me your love;
take me to the checkout, make me strong.
Rukshana, Queen of Healing, Lady of
the Paracetamol all dressed in white,
indulge me. Tell me I will be alright.

Sonnet XXXII   23rd April 2020

'Social Disruption will last for at least a year' – Daily Telegraph

The whole of London's going for a run,
our artisanal cheese is under threat,
the queen has given up her birthday guns
while we are clapping for the NHS.
Everybody's buying underwear
and longlife milk, pyjamas, yeast and porn
online. Our fashion houses live in fear
of tracksuits as high-end shoppers mourn
deserted catwalks, oil prices tumble
into negative and Branson swings
a mortgage on his Caribbean isle.
We loosen up as April sunshine brings
the crowds; the parks and streets are rammed,
it's mayhem: we've rediscovered traffic jams.

Sonnet XXXIII   24th April 2020

'Coronavirus response chief Dr Deborah Birx looks stunned
as Trump suggests injecting disinfectant' – The Independent

The president has shamed you where it hurts:
in public. Why so quiet Doctor Birx?
You've lasted years! You do it for the perks
but now the blessing has become the curse.
You've learned to tolerate his kinks and quirks
to feed ambition or a thirsty purse
but do you really love him, Doctor Birx?
Your sycophantic soul still flirts
with fame, but suddenly you're risk-averse;
your eyes deny, you fudge the facts. What's worse,
the camera has caught you, Doctor Birx.
You try a range of faces; nothing works.
Behind this viral joke the terror lurks,
still you say nothing. Nothing, Doctor Birx.

Sonnet XXXIV 25th April 2020

'Ecuador: cardboard coffins distributed amid coronavirus fears' – The Guardian

The brokers love a long-stemmed rose; fêted,
big-bloomed icon of romance, plastic-sleeved
then packed in cardboard boxes, air-freighted
from Ecuador. That's how it was at least.
The fields are filled with flowers, harvest
of petalled fire yearning towards the sun,
but who will pick them now, long past their best?
They raise no revenue, their purpose gone,
their meaning lost. There's panic in the streets
and who needs flowers now the hospitals
cannot contain the dead? There's only grief
to guide the times; no wreath, no ritual,
but from the distant hills a white wind blows
the grace of flowers and the scent of rose.

Sonnet XXXV   26th April 2020

'So you made your own sourdough starter. Instead of a beautiful,
bouncy loaf, though, you got a lifeless, jaw-breaking cracker'
— Researchers at North Carolina State University

Of course the strategy's a scam. We longed
for leadership and faith, not floury nights
in kitchens kneading bread. We blundered on,
they did not save us. We tried the rise,
we proved the dough, with short supplies of trust
we fed the promise, but it did not grow.
Believe the glory of the coming crust!
A miracle will spread from what we know,
the scummy bastards cried. Without a plan
their ignorance was manifest. They spent
our children's futures. We tried to tell them *Man,*
your bread is death, give us some nourishment.
We hoped they'd stop; instead, they went too far.
We should not be surprised and yet we are.

Sonnet XXXVI   27th April 2020

*'As we've globalised and invaded natural habitats – that's
what's created the increased risk, not the animals themselves'*
– The Independent

Here at the entrance, you can watch the bats
at dusk. The overhanging bamboo trees
sway like a curtain and then, just like that,
from the cave's dark mouth, one creature streaks
skywards; then thousands of tiny, winged gods
follow, preparing for the night-time shift.
I've never really known a bat, it's hard
to love a flying rodent apt to drop its shit
on you, one who eats its body weight
in bugs and carries poison in its blood.
But listen! Watch! Maybe it's not too late
to find some bat-respect; they look so good,
tiny black arrows painting zig-zag lines
across the firmament, singing as they fly.

Sonnet XXXVII   28th April 2020

'Most of the pangolin skins exported between 1975 and 2000
went to North America, where they were turned into handbags,
belts, wallets, and fancy cowboy boots' – The New Yorker

Near-biped wanderer, hands clasped in front
as if in contemplation, you could be
my long-lost sister. Tacky-tongued,
endangered and lactating deity,
built to roll, not run, oblivious
to our schemes, you sport your scales like medals.
Sister, they're useless; we'll have you. Toothless
source of revenue, red-listed mammal,
trafficked victim of the bogus trade
in mortal myth, beware the marketplace.
Boiled alive, descaled, bagged-up and graded,
you yield a bitter meat, the markets claim.
We bring you to the table just the same.

Sonnet XXXVIII   29th April 2020

'Boris Johnson and fiancée announce birth of son' – BBC News

'It is believed that the prime minister has seven children, however he has not officially confirmed the exact number' – The Independent

Any farm would welcome him; potent
and exact with his ejaculate.
A specimen who cares not what he's spent
in spunk or where it went, he'll mate
with any willing hen he finds on heat,
comes on repeat, he's prone to populate
whole dynasties with his tenacious seed;
foul breeding stock, explosive, indiscreet.
Today's tricky; handily, he's on retreat
minding the chick, not the affairs of state,
tip-top excuse for missing the debate.
In lieu of leader we must contemplate
this total cock who postures, struts and whines
inside the henhouse, ducking question time.

Sonnet XXXIX   30ᵗʰ April 2020

'Coronavirus: Tube may be 'overwhelmed'
when lockdown is lifted, report warns' – BBC

Come on, who didn't hate the Central Line,
that smug red seam that cuts a curse across
the nodal map, harbourer of grime
and sweat and tunnels, haven for the rats?
And who would want it back? Who didn't dread
the morning shuffle, O god, armpit,
body against body, rank descent
into commuter hell, lurch of the lift?
Who'd call the demon home? Who'd want to rouse
the old gods from their sleep, revive the rituals
of push and progress, catch the sliding doors?
I would. My body aches, I am all animal;
I crave the touch and chaos of the life
that's gone, I miss the closeness of the tribe.

Sonnet XL 1ˢᵗ May 2020

'*Coronavirus: Trump stands by China lab origin theory for virus*' – BBC

'*Meitner had two difficulties: She was a Jew living as an exile in Sweden because of the Jewish persecution going on in Nazi Germany, and she was a woman ... Meitner's contributions to nuclear physics were never recognized by the Nobel committee*' –*Massive Science*

Podcasts! They channel pain. I can't believe
this story. I'm pretty porous, I admit,
sobbing on my daily walk ambushed by grief.
I'm crying for a long-dead physicist
or is she an excuse? It's hard to know
when everything connects to everything:
that's physics isn't it? The world implodes
and Meitner's life is in my ears; that queen
of fission and regret, who wouldn't bend
her truth to help create the atom bomb.
Is this her moral compass in my hand?
I can't see it. Maybe my eyes are wrong.
The sky thickens with cloud, the podcast ends,
I head on homewards as the dark descends.

Sonnet XLI   2nd May 2020

*'Death Map. Interactive coronavirus map lets you
find out number of deaths in your postcode'* – The Sun

And suddenly it's Fear. He wakes me up
at odd hours, pulls me out of bed,
he works by stealth, he spikes my morning cup
with dark. I drink him like a drug, I dread
his silences. Fear speaks in chokes. He knows
no tongue. He knows no end. Today I caught
his ratchet scratch inside my head. *Hello
dear Fear,* I said. *What news?* Fear took out
his flashcards, shuffled them. *PLAGUE* said one.
STARVATION said the next. *LIFE JACKETS. LOCUSTS.
BROKEN HOSPITALS. TYRANTS. GUNS.
Stop! I cried.* Fear's eyes rolled in their sockets.
He raised another card. *YOUR CHILDREN. Oh shit,*
I said. Fear took a little bow and on he went.

Sonnet XLII   3rd May 2020

'Warren Buffett dumps US airline stocks, saying
'world has changed' after Covid-19' – BBC News

The Oracle of Omaha has rocked
the markets, he's let his darlings fall,
he's caved and dumped his sagging stocks
in grounded birds, he's smashed his crystal ball,
he's torn up his portfolio and left us
flightless. Warren, what the hell? You said
you knew! You said that we could trust
our well-oiled wings and so we did.
Warren, we fuelled up our death machines,
we burned a trail, we turned the sky to ash,
we owned the heavens, lived the human dream,
displaced the angels as we risked the crash,
we held dominion over earth and air,
we flew. Yeah, Warren, we were gods up there.

Sonnet XLIII   4th May 2020

'Coronavirus: Bikers fined for 200-mile fish and chips trip' – BBC News

Today's revelation is a recipe
for corpulence. Well, aren't they all
these days? Fat and sugar, crazy
creaming of the love, the boil of hateful oil,
rolling the dough, dunking the dips.
Who knew the arcane joys of baking days,
distraction cookies, spill of chocolate chips
could really do it; help to hold the lie
in place. I sense my body's not my own.
I'm spreading out, part woman, part batter,
googling the sweet stuff safe at home,
growing softer, blinder, badder, fatter.
My heart expands, I rail inside my skin,
I keep the horror out, I stuff the comfort in.

Sonnet XLIV   5th May 2020

'Coronavirus: UK death toll passes Italy to be highest in Europe' – BBC News

So dead is a real word, like bread, or night,
or sex. The spectre in a baleful dress
breaks in and hangs about the house. He bites
your ankles, tugs your chain, he bares his chest
and howls. Dead: it's just a word although
it turns out to be solid; like steel or stones
or gold. You'd think that I would know by now:
we go to ground like rain, yes everyone.
The doctors and the nurses always knew.
They never kept it from us but we left them
to it. Dead. The real deal, close and true.
Our mortal coils are busting overtime.
Dead. Who wants to give the wheel a spin?
We all know someone. Dead. That word again.

Sonnet XLV   6ᵗʰ May 2020

'Police should consider action against Neil Ferguson over lockdown breach, Matt Hancock suggests' – The Daily Telegraph

'Professor Lockdown quits over trysts' – Daily Mail

It's clickbait, windup, focus and distract:
fabulous mantra. Britain's in the mood
for trouser-farce again, man trapped
behind his own facade. Oh Prof, true dude
of science, pimped out to the brotherhood
of *fuck-it while you can,* your hands are tied,
they've fleeced you, Prof, they've thrown you to the wolves,
they've conjured up a storm where headlines rise
and carry you to infamy, leaving your quest
submerged and murky. Who cares what we've got
or how to cure it? Note how the press
go fishing, sell the catch as if it's hot
and fresh. It's circuses and sourdough, Prof,
go home, bend over, take your trousers off.

Sonnet XLVI 7th May 2020

'We've come under what could have been a vast peak, as though we've going through some huge Alpine tunnel and we can now see the sunlight and pasture ahead of us' – Boris Johnson, BBC News

How can we change our lives, we ponder, as
we walk the thin canal path. It's been good
so far, we're at the hottest year on record,
spring of bird and water. What lucky chance
gave birth to us between the darknesses,
the plagues and wars, loved and unblooded,
safe? So far. We know our little wounds
are nothing anymore. It's been a blast,
sweetheart. We know we can't go back. We hold
the knowledge like a bomb between us, fake
a future, work the promise of the world,
as if there were an answer and an end
to this. We share our burden; take the weight
of unexploded hope into our hands.

Sonnet XLVII   8th May 2020

'Solemnity and celebration as Britain pays VE Day tribute to war generation' – The Guardian

I'd seen the bunting but I was well surprised
to hear the screech of airborne terror.
History repeats, birdsong is split and shattered,
obliteration of the day, the sound of Spitfires
celebrating. Look up! First nothing, then
the flying V loops overhead to scrawl
its coloured vapour trails across the heavens.
The neighbours sing with Vera, engines roar
red, white and blue, the people wave
their flags, drink pick-me-ups for victory.
Horror hides behind a wall of noise
bolstered by cheering, scones and English tea.
Only the silence matters; the dead are here
always: Auschwitz, Stalingrad, Hiroshima.

Sonnet XLVIII   9th May 2020

No 'Single leap to freedom, minister warns' – BBC News

'Government scientists have condemned a "Stalinist" attempt to censor Covid-19 advice' – The Week Daily Briefing

Our home is its own universe: one sews,
one cooks, one writes, one sings. Ephemeral,
the wonder of this cottage industry;
we are become small gods between four walls.
Today we're making animals; yesterday
we painted sky, tomorrow we'll be free
for planting seeds of hope and rendezvous
with doves and arguments about the news.
But we're not really gods. We're just a mess
of rage and faith. We join the daily queues
for truth, we read the sacred books, make time
for havoc, sip the gin, crash through the stress
of what and wherefore in an endless sequence
as we fall apart, reload, re-love, rewind.

Sonnet XLIX 10th May 2020

'Stay alert. Control the Virus. Save Lives' – UK Government

'All devolved nations reject new coronavirus slogan' – The Guardian

My honourable friends, we've got a grip.
Whoo-hoo! We'll put the public on divert
with yellow, added bits of green, we'll flip
the message and for best results, insert
a meaningless instruction. It's leadership!
Fluff up the rhetoric and thus assert
authority, invoke the spirit of the blitz,
A conga line, a slogan, short and curt
in upper case. It's bloody science, folks.
Be vigilant. Let's catch the little squirt!
For ladies: shove some Dettol up your skirt;
gentlemen, pistols at dawn. STAY ALERT,
eyes peeled for particles. Friends, there is hope.
Man the cannons, load up your microscopes.

Sonnet L   11th May 2020

'New York warns of children's illness linked to Covid-19 after three deaths' – The Guardian

'Conception is a sin, Birth is pain, Life is toil, Death a necessity'
– After Salvator Rosa's 'L'Umana Fragilita' 1656

Death takes centre stage, experienced,
adept, emerging from the dark: wing, skull
and grin. The baby boy, obedient,
surely not literate, is writing, quill
in hand, as Death dictates. The ink is on the page:
the mother reads; boy gathered on her lap.
She knows she will not save him from the plague.
We call it history, but see, snap-snap!
Death comes again. We think we've beaten him
but find he owns the street, the shop, the school,
the theatre, hospital and birthing room.
In this deluded age, the leading role
is ours, we think. Nah. We're just the cameo.
Death takes the curtain call and steals the show.

Sonnet LI   12th May 2020

*'People in England will be able to spend more time outdoors
from Wednesday "for leisure purposes"'* – BBC News

I often try to write about the coots
and fail. Perhaps they have a message but
I'm just a visitor. The chicks were cute
but now they're squabbling, gangly, caught out
by unexpected adolescence, mum and dad
still busy all the time, augmenting the nest,
diving for weeds, guarding the brood.
Is this activity profound, maybe a test
of my ability with metaphors?
Apparently it's rare for all to grow
to adulthood, what with the swans, the drains,
the heat, polluted water. I don't know
how to help; some days I stop and count.
Sometimes I care, sometimes I don't.

Sonnet LII   13th May 2020

'*Long queues force Elgin Burger King to close as police called in*' – BBC News

I have learned canals can be a home
for coots, that coots have fascinating feet,
their noisy chicks might well provoke the swans
to rage; that diners prize the roasted civet,
for its meat and some may ask to view
the pangolin alive before it's slaughtered;
that everything exists to be consumed;
that even flesh of bat can be endured
if you are into it, that queues along
the highway are insane, because, we've heard,
Burger King has opened up again;
that we are nothing like the waterbirds
who rear their young and make their nests,
take only what they need and leave the rest.

Sonnet LIII   14th May 2020

'Normal People delivers best week ever for BBC 3' – The Guardian

'What they have now they can never have back again'
– Normal People, Sally Rooney

After a normal day of woe and webinar,
of handwash, googlemuse and interwhinge,
we sip our normal wine with dinner
and normally collapse onto the sofa
logged-out, tuned in. Mostly we binge
on something lost. It's been a million years
since gym-fit bodies shared their normal beds
in Tuscan villas with their grubby friends
or got depressed on college campuses,
in bars, consulted shrinks in actual rooms
on bondage sex and academic brilliance,
mourned at funerals, never kept a distance.
Remember it? The shock of skin and shame,
nostalgic, reckless days of normal pain.

Sonnet LIV   15th May 2020

*'Exact day UK will have zero coronavirus
deaths – predicted by experts' – The Daily Star*

Perception flips. The isolated heart
plays tricks. Today's the same as yesterday
but not. At intervals along the path I spot
a stream of people, paper cups displayed:
time travel. The old world beckons like a dream.
Just give me one barista in a fug
of steaming crowds, froth and caffeine.
The scent of freedom rises like a drug.
I change my route, I walk the cobbled ways
of Wapping looking for my life. The past
has shut its doors but the old coffee place
is half alive with hipster peeps in masks
and gloves. *One In, One Out* the sign proclaims.
I buy, I sip, it doesn't taste the same.

Sonnet LV   16th May 2020

'We owe it to the children to open schools'
– Gavin Williamson, Education Secretary

Who sends their children off to school? Who puts
their packages in quarantine? Who trusts
the fakers on TV? I don't know, caught
between denial and abandon, I must
start washing my bananas, cut my hair,
not get twitchy at the little signs
of hope and promise. There's nothing there.
We bump and falter, read between the lines,
we share our little bubble with its air
that smells of soap, our charming sphere
of hope and faith. It's really nice in here;
our slack beliefs are such a comfort, sure
as dirt. *Stay home, go out, do as you're told,*
your call, be close but stand apart   o god

Sonnet LVI 17ᵗʰ May 2020

'Britain on fast track to virus recovery' – Sunday Express

I'm lost, the daily entry still unwritten,
a fractious day reaching its close. I sit
and slump and scratch my life, submitting
to the possible: the empty page. Dammit.
But look! The morning walk rolls in, the song
of tree and bird is working in my ear,
duck eggs are hatching underneath the sun
and I remember poetry's a form of prayer.
I bless this room, this pen, this wooden stool,
I bless the struggle and the inner light,
my absent gods, my disbelieving soul,
my heart in freefall and the hands that write
the loosening, the body's sure revolt
against the mind. These tears: salt. Sweet. Salt.

Sonnet LVII   18th May 2020

'Erupting during the final stages of World War I, this global disaster
reinforced the era's nihilism and apocalyptic visions of despair'

After Edvard Munch's 'Self portrait with Spanish Flu', 1919

This is a space we dare not enter: see
the artist in the foreground seated in
his sickly yellow chair, the rotted green
of spill and slick. The sickroom spins
its palette in a colour wheel of dread,
the self as subject is awake, a mess
of fever sheets behind him on the bed
where currents seethe and ebb, delirious
with pain. The artist turns his sunken eyes
towards us, opening his mouth to speak
in blurs and gasps, in fallen daubs and sighs.
This kinless captain of the catastrophic
asks for nothing, paints in queasy tones,
reminds us that we live and die alone.

Sonnet LVIII   19th May 2020

'UK Death toll hits 35,000 and jobless claims soar' – BBC News

The city green is colonised by men
squatting on the turf with mansize weights:
topless men in shorts; men who bend
and lift, men with pheromones on dates
with varied vibes of masculinity.
Oh Man, eyeball those men over there
stacking their dumbells to infinity,
aspiring, heaving gods of sweat and hair
who lift a little more each day. Keep lifting!
Muscle up and build your manly chests
and your delusions. The sky is sinking;
you think you'll take the weight, you Atlases,
you Titans, but that's just a myth: alas,
you're only human like the rest of us.

Sonnet LIX   20th May 2020

'Europe should brace for second wave' says EU coronavirus Chief'
– The Guardian

Remember Brick Lane Sundays? Bagel bake,
garam masala, artisan baristas,
sellers of hip and vintage on the make,
the smell of weed, the Sunday lager drinkers,
trestle tables, strangers skin to skin,
the men who stood outside the curry houses
flaunting menus, beckoning you in,
how you walked by, assailed by choice?
Remember Shadwell station and the sight
of dealers on the corner, fried chicken round
the clock, the homeless begging late at night,
how you never liked the Overground?
Remember how you wished the world would change?
Remember when the trains were just the trains?

Sonnet LX   21st May

'World sees highest daily increase in virus cases' – BBC News

*'Jessie Dawson sits among mannequins occupying some tables
so diners will not feel isolated by coronavirus distancing measures
when The Inn at Little Washington'* – REUTERS/Kevin Lamarque

Where did they find these lifeless mannequins
from another era? The chap with waxen face,
straw boater at an awkward angle, manspreading
for his partner dummy, foreground, veiled in lace
fascinator and frock. Who'd want to join
these zombie freaks for a hot date, converse
over *Foie Gras, Lobster, Baby Lamb Loin,
Lilliputian Dreamsicle dessert*?
What Frankenstein designed that stiff who stares
into the distance, posturing behind them?
Let's not pretend: even the silverware
looks more alive than these sad specimens
who are the opposite of hope; endgame
for the only, lonely human in the frame.

Sonnet LXI   22nd May 2020

'Weekly tribute to coronavirus key workers as UK
gathers again to Clap for our Carers' – ITV

Should we or should we not? Our little isle
is quietly divided. Thursday nights,
most gather at their windows, British-style
and let the carers know they care. However trite
and sticky we may feel with awkward spoon
on saucepan, making noises seems to matter
somehow, somewhere, but to whom?
Here's to rainbows, hearts and clappers,
centenarians who do their laps,
nurses and their freebie Krispy Kremes,
to fireworks, death defying, cheesy thanks,
morale! Let's find a way to keep the dream.
I daren't mention circuses or bread;
we'd surely spot that kind of scam, and yet –

Sonnet LXII   23rd May 2020

'*White House Military Office members clean a staircase for Air Force One in Allentown, Pennsylvania. (AP Photo Evan Vucci)*' 23rd May

'U.S. DEATHS NEAR 100,000, AN INCALCULABLE LOSS' – New York Times

The green is calling. The president must play!
His blank-eye lackeys, armed with muscles, guns
and dusters mount red stairs that stretch away
into the blue, awaiting Airforce One.
These military men trained up for combat
get domestic: they disinfect and buff
with sweet commitment for the plutocrat
dictator hooked on downtime at the club.
What greater purpose for the nation's jet
than ferrying a villain in a leading role
to stride the fairway – weekends spent
at hitting balls into their tiny holes,
the comfort of meaningless victories?
Meanwhile, the hate ferments, the virus breeds.

Sonnet LXIII   24th May 2020

'*Caring for your wife and child is not a crime*' – Michael Gove

'*Several Conservative MPs have called for the PM's chief adviser Dominic Cummings to quit, amid claims he broke coronavirus lockdown rules*' – BBC News

Downing Street does its best to blag but lacks
the teat of milky slogans, usually on tap.
It's worrying. Robbed of his starring role
their *Weirdo Misfit* can't Take Back Control.
Where is the Big Man's voice? Downing Street's
cracked facade denies, retracts and tweets:
*It's not a crime to feed your helpless wife
and babe in arms, to take a little drive ...*
But who would suckle on those frozen tits
again? Boris? He whines through thirsty grin
and rotten teeth, he slurps a curdled hit
of risk: his man, still pregnant with advice
just balls his fist and rolls the magic dice
of rhetoric: this time they do not spin.

Sonnet LXIV 25th May 2020

'*Boris backs No 10 svengali who flouted
PM's own strict lockdown rules*' – The Daily Mail

I'm nearly feeling sorry that I had
a go at Dominic. Amid the hate,
I should be kind, he's just a worried Dad
who's being savaged on the internet
for doing what so many do, bending
the rules a little bit. *We've all been lax
and yet #cummingsmustgo is trending*
the kind ones say, *who hasn't made mistakes?*

Hang on. Our architect of discontent,
our surly sloganeer, our king of spin,
our new Rasputin with his lies for rent
confesses nothing, holds his ground, digs in,
prepares to fall and rise and fall and rise
in endless resurrections. Watch this space.

Sonnet LXV   26th May 2020

'WHO *halts trials of* Hydroxychloroquine *because of safety fears*' – BBC News

Hydroxychloroquine: if only.
Our hopes rush in and hang about like bad friends
bearing bad drugs, looking for the money.
We need a vaccine for the toxic mind,
the tribal rage, the politics of fear.
The weather's beautiful and gangs of boys
are laughing in the world's bright gaze, dealers
line the streets and hawk their brand of joy:
quick silver bullets, needles, guns and spit.
The men are pissing on the public lawns
and human ignorance is infinite;
our grand resolve is melting in the sun.
Heads up! The plague is dancing in the streets.
My daughter is still coughing. It's been weeks.

Sonnet LXVI 27th May 2020

'Amazon under threat: Fires, loggers and now virus' – BBC

suppose the flowers clogged the logging roads
suppose the oil inside the wells foreclosed
the world's lungs weren't on fire suppose
the trucks were stuck or let's get rid of those
impose a status on the worms a temple
to the toads worship the bees & bicycles
& grope for bouts of light where nothing grows
dose up with ragwort pigweed every mode
of weed suppose we fled the fisheries
& shared the loaves suppose the CEOs
took off their dirty clothes I don't suppose
bat or pangolin will note our batshit hopes
we're on the ropes but just suppose who knows
suppose a new suppose see where it goes

Sonnet LXVII   28th May 2020

*'Medical staff at the Royal London Hospital say
a rise in cases is inevitable'* – BBC

*'The light can absolutely alter the manner in which your
selfie appears either adversely or positively'* – *toptenreviews*

The nurse unfolds the white dividing screen;
and disappears behind it. Hers is a final face,
a final hand to hold in this last stopping place.
Amid the blue-tinged loss, a chaplain recites
the last balm for the dying: *There is no god
but God.* I turn off to shop online for light.
I need it. Don't we all want to be seen,
beloved and delivered, held and blessed?
I face myself, my wrinkles well in shot.
Oh, conundrum, gruesome selfie minefield
browsing the choices: *midday sun, moon-cold spill*,
illuminate me as I live – and all the while
the dead arrive at darkened morgues; unreal,
too real, cold in their berths of shining steel.

Sonnet LXVIII   29ᵗʰ May 2020

'Cities across the US were convulsed by protests on Thursday night over the police killing of George Floyd, a 46-year old black man'
– The Guardian

'When the looting starts, the shooting starts' – Walter Headley, Miami Police Chief, Dec 1967 Donald Trump, 29th May 2020

George Floyd: if not me, then who? If
a white cop puts his knee on a black man's neck,
if the black man says *I can't breathe*, dare I speak?
Is it my place? Let's talk history and grief
and rage, let's talk trade. Race. Slavery.
George Floyd *could not breathe*. A white man
murdered him, a cop in uniform:
no noose, no gun: just bone, muscle and knee –
when the looting starts, the shooting starts –
he dug in hard, bore down, he played his part,
the lyncher baying at the lynching tree.
If I keep silent this time, shame on me,
white woman at my desk inventing rhymes
for this   there is no rhyme for this

Sonnet LXIX   30ᵗʰ May 2020

'... losing (Cummings) as an adviser and an ally would be
a severe blow to Mr Johnson' – BBC News

After 'Bonaparte visiting the victims of the plague at Jaffa,
March 11 1799' by Antoine-Jean Gros

Now, strike a pose that says you're not to blame.
Trust my vision, I'm your only friend.
For authenticity, forgive me, I have stained
your breeches, left your cummerbund distressed.
The centre of the picture is the place to stand
for maximum results. And do not push
the message, just a simple laying on of hands,
ungloved – ungloved! – christ-like, to touch
the man who lifts his putrid arm. We'll bend
the truth to prop the myth, suggest you care.
I'll paint you in, although it never happened.
I'll sketch the dead and dying here and there,
but shadowed; you, their hero, in the light
with just a red-plumed hat for extra height.

Sonnet LXX   31st May 2020

'*Two crises convulse a nation: A Pandemic and Police Violence*' – New York Times

Everyone is sacred, the singers always say,
along with other stuff like *Keep a hold on love
whatever madness turns your love away,
don't give in to despair, never give up.*
We're doting on the curve, we plot the dots
and count in abstract numbers while the hospitals
submerge, the planet lurches, drowns and clots.
We're locking down, we're breaking out, we still
don't know our enemy. We're turning on each other,
rage and bullets, teargas and despair.
Cops load their guns and super-spreaders gather.
Are we more stupid than we were before?
Where is our memory? Maybe it doesn't matter.
Love's lost its glamour, nobody's sacred anymore.

Sonnet LXXI   1ˢᵗ June 2020

'Outdoor markets and car showrooms can now resume trading,
provided they have Covid-related safety measures in place' – BBC News

The dress doesn't fit. I'm not surprised.
Nothing fits these days and the first courage
flattens, the old life shimmers like a mirage.
I fill in the return; nothing's a normal size,
some things you can't do virtually, I write,
I don't know how to send it back. Who's in charge
of this debacle? This sorry garment, crushed
and boxed, awaits redemption. Please advise.
The past is in the post office. I know the way
but all the streets have lost their names. Too late
to fix, the hours and days are out to play,
the gates are open, girls in ragged frocks
are kissing in the parks. How to translate
this falling city; blunder, quake and aftershocks.

Sonnet LXXII   2nd June 2020

'Tear gas used to disperse protesters in enabling President Trump to walk to a church to pose for photos' – BBC News

Imagine that the Evil walks amongst us
in plain sight, Bible in his right hand, say,
a perfect prop, ribbon of red dripping
from its pages in the humid evening.
How teargas loves a crowd, he says. Let's play.
Who doesn't love a lachrymator? Let's
call a drowning where this awesome powder
hits the skin and bonds with human sweat.

Get it? The Evil preaching to the choir?
Say it couldn't happen here. Imagine
if it could. The streets erupt, the storm begins,
the Evil raises hell and fans the fire
with God's book. The screaming streets run mad,
the Evil spreads his poisoned gas. Imagine that.

Sonnet LXIII   3rd June 2020

'Will hairdressers really reopen on July 4?' – Daily Telegraph

It was early March, just a dream ago
I last sat in that chair when hair mattered
and chatted about this and that. *So, Matteo*
I asked. *How are things in Italy?* He cleared
his throat and laughed. *Business is picking up,*
he said, feathering my fringe into my eyes.
My Papa's still at work, living above the shop,
Lockdown? Not a problem. He snipped and smiled.
Family business, he giggled, looking smug.
Hair? I asked. *No no*, he answered. *Undertakers.*
He asked about my holidays. I shrugged.
Sicily is nice he said, turning on the shaver,
his warm breath on my neck. Did I laugh?
It seemed funny at the time. Now, not so much.

Sonnet LXIV   4th June 2020

*'Vladimir Putin has ordered a state of emergency after 20,000 tonnes
of diesel fuel spilled into a river inside the Arctic Circle' – The Guardian*

Yesterday was hope and possibility,
today is oil and Arctic, knees on throats,
tomorrow will be faith and cake, maybe
a bit of yoga; next week will be stay afloat
or stay in bed. Today is stay intact don't let
the body fall apart, the anger turned to dread,
the diesel and the roubles do the cover-up.
Put down your copper-eating phone
stop clicking like you'll find some helpful clues,
don't mine for answers. What do you use
for comfort when the world is comfortless,
the slick subdues the river, just read the fucking news?
Don't feel sorry for yourself, lose the hair shirt,
get up, get clean, get dressed, get on with it.

Sonnet LXV   5th June 2020

'UK *passes 40,000 Coronavirus deaths*' – BBC *News*

The Sad is feeling it today, it's had enough.
The Sad is feeling bad for being sad, but no,
don't talk at the Sad and tell it to buck up
when the Sad is falling into its own shadow.
Don't give the Sad the third degree. It runs
with pain, it bonds with fear and faith, it gets
to grips, applies the balm of sorrow to its own
beleaguered eyes. The Sad will not accept
comparisons, knows only soft strands
of itself, the briny reaches of the soul.
The Sad understands; it lies down in the hot land
of the heart and weeps: it keeps you whole,
it does the human work. Hold tight. Believe
the Sad, give it some air and let it breathe.

Sonnet LXVI   6th June 2020

'*German man is suspect in case of Madeleine McCann*' – New York Times

Maddie's hit the headlines yet again,
her parents ageing while she stays the same.
The footage is familiar but our grief
has aged and petrified: pink rabbit
in a photograph, a mother tight with pain.
Who could move on? Not the papers, drawn
forever back to this, an easy hit
in complicated times; a life long gone,
an unsolved loss that garners sympathy.
Weirdly, we're comforted, our world re-framed
by wholesome sorrow, innocence regained,
no need to take a stance; no collective loss.
We read and tut while Maddie's errant eye,
singular, remote, is watching us.

Sonnet LXVII   7th June 2020

'Police horse bolts as London anti-racism protest turn violent' – Daily Mail

' ... peaceful protests swell nationwide' – New York Times

Johnson plays with thunder
Hancock plays the fool
Trump is in his bunker
Cummings digs a hole

One hand on the Bible
and one hand on the gun
the minders faff and fiddle
but their long white day is done

The Chief of Staff is bloated
in the mansion of the flies
his rats are running rabid
his pigmen soil their sty

and the stable horse has bolted
with teargas in its eye

Sonnet LXVIII   8th June 2020

'*Shielding for at-risk groups to stay in place until July 31*' – Sky News

It's like living underwater, swaying, soft
and silenced in the green whoosh where days
become un-navigable continents.
How many of the shielded take their place
on some strange seabed, their nights untethered,
only their calendars and telephones
to find their bearings. Their inner weather
changeable, their destinies unknown,
they bob and suffer, weakened by the sludge
of months. The doctor writes the medicine,
the postman leaves the letters, but it's no-touch
for the shielded ones. O, strange new discipline,
this distance between us, drifting through brine
and fog; you in your ocean, me in mine.

Sonnet LXIX   9th June 2020

'Hey, there are swans out here' – River and Sky

Today I tuned out – turned off the noise
& let the voices drop and drift
I cleared a space away from sound
& sickness & came to silence

I can now confirm
           there's not much
              happening here
just a slowing of the pulse & a flicker
of luminescence in the interior

            friends, joyously, I bring
no news, except how silver is the midday light
&: I may as well bless this glass of clean water
perched on my desk &: the accompanying miracle
lemon-slice with its intricate yellow membranes
its bitter pith its carpels & vesicles &
this sudden, attainably slakeable thirst

Sonnet LXXX 10th June 2020

'People think it's over but it's not' – BBC News

I want my old life back; friends on the clock,
the scrum of tables tight with lunches,
hustle and rush of days. No-one touches
anymore, we bluster, thunderstruck
through our loneliness, we try our luck
with myths and mantras, we learn to crush
the urge to hug or take a hand, we push
the boundaries when all the gates are shut;

all but yours, my friend, that day we stole
a morning in your garden: blue pot of tea,
the grey mist, chat and spatter of the rain.
There was cake and seeing you was beautiful
in three dimensions; a life almost regained;
so close to freedom, but not exactly free.

Sonnet LXXXI 11ᵗʰ June 2020

*'I didn't contribute anything to it, other than standing guard.
But I was forced to do it, it was an order'* – Bruno Dey, a former
SS watchman at his trial.

Slipped under the radar, back pages, smart,
embattled, the old man shrinks and mopes
in his wheelchair. Justice has been halted
and restarted like a bad car, it chokes
on its own gas. This is not a time to share
more Jewish news, some might say; the trial
of a Nazi in his *Autumn years,* papped here,
face hidden behind a bright blue file.
The wheels move slow, it's getting late;
the perpetrator's half-asleep, doolally,
propped up in the back beside the greasy body
of complicity, desperate and fake
knowing that history, that slimy bureaucrat,
can turn. Our fallen statues tell us that.

Sonnet LXXXII 12th June 2020

*'Social and family groups are complicated
and might not fit bubble rules'* – BBC News

In flux and disarray, the normal falls,
the social bubbles burst, the air
is soap and fumes. Your ragged hair
is in your eyes. Look up! Someone calls
from a high window, climbing the walls.
Buy a pouffe! she says. Is that your mother
risen from the dead talking about furniture?
Clean lines, she says. *Keep it simple*.

She buys you a red dress. Sixteen.
You can't keep your distance as she zips
you in. *The party's off* you say. *No way*,
she cries, holding you, lonely in her dream
of this no-touch summer. Dirty as a sigh,
lipsticked, she paints a long-forgotten kiss.

Sonnet LXXXIII   13th June 2020

'Greene King Pubs to open with perspex screens and controlled toilets'
– The Guardian

When all the grief is over we should throw
a giant fuck-off party with balloons
and tenderness, smooch under the moon,
live it up skin to skin and grow
our own, get high with everyone we know,
share the plate and pass around the spoon,
gather face-to-face, give up on Zoom
and live the actual life, turn off our phones
revert to calling cards and charabancs,
smoke signals, yoghurt pots and string.
Let's kiss strangers, give the weeds a chance,
green the streets together, offer thanks
and build some bridges, those lovely things
that everyone's allowed to walk across.

Sonnet LXXXIV   14th June 2020

'We are so sorry to announce this, but we are going to have to cancel Glastonbury 2020' – Glastonbury Festival Website

The toss and heat of tents pitched so close
you could hear your neighbours breathing; sleepless
wanderings, the tripping women wearing wings
and learning how to fly. Let's raise a toast
to mingled mud and sweat and dust,
to shared release, to golden nights of flings
and visions in the fields of touch and green,
miracles round every corner, finding your kin
inside the music. Dog-tired, dirty, human,
dancing close-up with half a million
others. Remember that? The weariness,
the portaloos, the burger stands, the voices
raised in song, the technicolour charms
of long-lost strangers opening their arms.

Sonnet LXXXV   15ᵗʰ June 2020

'*Six thousand people attend two illegal raves in Greater Manchester*'
— *The Guardian*

Runners create their own slipstream and
the morning after a hot night, the street
is stocked with trash and broken glass and
parks are plastic-spread, the hi-vis fleet
commands the trash, the raves rage on and
the latest from Atlanta's bad. Who needs
another death report but this won't stop and
death takes on a bland taste as it bleeds
in graphics told in black and bullet and
the cult of gun and gas and sweat and heat
another peak of *where are we now* and
disbelief and the kingpin crazies feed
their factories of flies with dirty cans
of gob and ash god help us all and and and

Sonnet LXXXVI   16th June 2020

'Britons risk being shut out of Europe over quarantine and infection rate'
— The Guardian

This year someone papped the lockdown dolphins,
canals false blue, sea mammals leaping free,
nature recreated as if in a new Eden.
I needed miracles, so I believed.
Remember our enchanted week in Venice,
lost and golden city? We'd waited years
for it, we ignored polluted waterways,
cruise-ship tours, churning mud, fake gondoliers.
I can't stop thinking of the *pesco frito;* hauls
of *fresh fish from the lagoon, catch of the day,*
they said, *precious, worth it, local.*
We fell for them, those deathly plates
of sadness, tiny motherless creatures, fresh
and battered, dredged from the depths.

Sonnet LXXXVII   17th June 2020

'The value of not having your life planned out' – BBC video by Brendan Miller

There are certain things you're not allowed
to talk about. Like: *where would you ever*
wear that dress again? or: *you may never*
tour Europe on a train, sweat with the crowd
in stadiums or: *we don't know how*
to hold this grief or: *better to live untethered*
from the old ways or: *things may change forever.*
You must not tell your children this. Your doubts
are not for them; leave them to hope. Don't say
it's over; drop your pessimism at
the door and roll in, cheerful, underplay
the panic, give them the happy chat,
unfold the future, trust the youthful dream,
gag the demons, let the children sing.

Sonnet LXXXVIII   18th June 2020

*'The singer of 'We'll Meet Again', who entertained troops
in World War Two, has died'* – BBC News

The anthropologists will have their day,
history will come for us. We don't know what
we're living through, we see only how high
the walls, how fake the news, how deep the rut.
We dizzy in our twisting narratives,
we try to find the light, our working heads
knock out a plot. There isn't one. Our gifs
are all we've got and Vera Lynn is dead;
end of an era, myth of a common cause
and what's the bloody point of art? Oh please!
Who else will tell the whip and wheeze? Our loss
must not be of imagination; the libraries
of the mind are open, the alchemy is strong,
the dark dream howls and shows its teeth. Bring it on.

Sonnet LXXXIX   19th June 2020

*'Brazil's Covid body collectors: 'SOS Funeral' is free for
all those who can't afford to pay for burials'* – BBC News

And suddenly it's tears, which is not the same
as sad; mawkish, often vacuous,
an ambush of the wet stuff, no warning.
What do I know of pain, my helpless, useless
weeping at the limp of an aged dog,
the sight of kids on swings behind the fence
designed to keep them out, a catalogue
of linen masks, all colours – *Soft*, it said –
just *Soft* and I was off. It feels so weird,
this failure of the heart to track and trace
the needy, cry when called. The cleansing tears
will not come out today, not even for Brazil
where bodies wait, grief stands at the gates
and pick-ups of the dead are free to all.

Sonnet XC   20th June 2020

*'Dearest Jacqueline: How time flies! I hope you have the
most lovely luscious lockdown birthday possible'* – Card from a friend

*'Soundlessly collateral and incompatible:
World is suddener than we fancy it'* – Louis MacNeice

The day was perfect and the working blue
was sky, the rise was in my heart, the clouds
could not eclipse the sun, oh glorious
the day, the louche of lounging, me and you,
the plural you; yes it was plural, true
but fragile, wrapped in the beauty of the *Us*,
and held there. Remember how it was:
the way the possible came through
and shone. A girl was doing cartwheels
on the lawn, somebody brought balloons.
The park glutted with roses, the green was real,
the London birds were singing birthday tunes.
Today we truly lived; fine band of revellers,
and made this history. Friends, it was fabulous.

Sonnet XCI   21ˢᵗ June 2020

'To break the pentameter, that was the first heave' – Ezra Pound

i dreamed all night of sonnets i nearly wrote
a whole one in my sleep i swear but now
i can't recall that i had anything to say let alone how
to keep the iamb in its hot hotel
of metre hey listen quick this sonnet's a bit shot
already awash with its insane rhymes so just as well
to claim the dissonance of these times to junk the rules
& find a fascist music a politics to cut
this metaphor with dust the world is on the turn it's chaos
the fat clock of the leadership is bust they left us
out of time and tools meanwhile here's me with my ridiculous trust
of form to hold the story & pitch the loss
but oh the frantic relief as i let the metre slide
shonkily to hell the scream is coming open wide

Sonnet XCII   22ⁿᵈ June 2020

'The pandemic is widening existing inequalities of wealth ...
lower income households are turning to borrowing, while many
higher income households, by contrast, have boosted their savings' – BBC News

'Christmas pantomimes are within weeks of being cancelled' – The Times

It's Monday and the news is in: someone
saw me MASTRUBATING (sic) and more
MALWARE, WEBCAM. If I don't pay, I'm done;
the MARKETS rally – why, why? – the poor
are FUCKED; the chancellor has had his fun
with FURLOUGHS and the money's GONE;
the SHOPS are full of stuff; no-one's short
of eggs; the weatherman parades the SUN;
the BAILIFFS are released! brace for the CUTS!
and mind the FOOD BANK! pull your socks up,
pull a pint; they're opening the PUBS my son;
PANTOMIMES are cancelled – that's a joke
ha-ha; the daily show goes on at shit o'clock.
Now slap your BRITISH THIGH and CARRY ON.

Sonnet XCIII   23rd June 2020

'*Lockdown relaxed in England ... Pubs, restaurants, hotels and hairdressers can open from 4th July*' – BBC News

The papers tell us things are looking up:
our vulnerable friends are good to go,
a fresh-air stroll, even a lucky trip
to *la-la-la*. The data softly folds,
hidden by wind and gabble. *All told,*
we've fixed a bubble; the lumpy numbers dip,
our bad boy's in retreat, foreswung. Hip-hip
nah-nah! Alertly taking back control
we dinkle in the dominax, the shield
and cooch is over. Rah-de-rah! We beat
the flictions. Only zaza dead! So neat
the sacrifuss. Truss up the doomish gong,
whizzo to the markets, dodgit clink and deal,
make moony! what could irkily go wrong?

Sonnet XCIV   24th June 2020

'Religion helped me through Lockdown' – BBC News

After Titian's Sisyphus (1548)

My love, for you I'd be a Sisyphus,
bent over with that boulder on his back,
chased by the hounds of hell and devil snake,
I'd cheat death and bear the consequences.
What's a bit of fire and toil compared
to what's at stake? Being alive is great:
let's try to stay that way. I want to wake
each morning next to you. I'd take a chance
on life, become a trickster just like him,
I'd risk forever badlands of the spirit
just to have some more of this: I'd wish
for one more fractious, high-end, limpid
lockdown day with you. Me, the atheist,
I'd fool the gods if I only believed in them.

Sonnet XCV   25th June 2020

'Secretary Robert Jenrick still has questions to answer over his role in a planning case involving Tory donor, (Richard Desmond)' – BBC News

'We don't want to give Marxists loads of doe for nothing' – Richard Desmond

I can satirise it all I like, but,
I tell myself, the virus isn't funny,
nor are The Commons and the money,
elected oafs with grubby fingers – butt,
class and misdemeanour. We know what
they pack inside their trouser pockets, chummy
with the porny fortunes of the low and scummy,
defending fiefdoms, trading up their smut
for favours; rotting MPs who work the bills
and fix the taxes, drink and stash together,
keep the *Marxists* off the *doe,* a screeching team
who crush our lives under their wings and juggle
us like eggs, who deal in nests and feathers,
pluck the chicks and strip the carcass clean.

Sonnet XCVI   26th June 2020

'A major incident was declared yesterday as thousands of people flocked to the seaside to enjoy the warm weather' – Daily Mirror

Come on Spotify, not him again. It's Billy Joel,
that tired old song, its well-worn punchline. Still,
I ache to hear him sing it: *making love
at midnight in the dunes* ... I'm thinking of
the beach today. Thousands of bodies, stacks
of melting chairs. Nobody has nobody's back,
the heat is on, to hell with staying in,
it's cross-the-line, it's spit and mayhem,
bring on the second wave. The headlines call
for punishment, the crowds ignore it all,
their forest of umbrellas stretches
across the sands, the Arctic Circle sweats
in heated editorials. I turn the page,
I stay at home, I sigh, I do not change.

Sonnet XCVII   27th June 2020

'*Coronavirus: Dentists warm of "severe damage" to patients*' – BBC News

Today a not-so-cool surprise upsets the flow.
Empathy, the world and all its suffering
recede. I'm hunting for a dentist, stuttering
my childhood terrors into the hopeful phone.
One front tooth, cracked. A constant busy tone.
I call again. It's such a tiny thing.
The world breaks, yet my circle of compassion
shrinks to me me me: flesh and bone.
Human, imperfect, angry, I lurch
inside myself, my courage now confined
to this. The bigger picture is too much
to even contemplate. Somebody come
and mend this broken mouth; I'm dumb
with rage and waiting. Who will fix my life?

Sonnet XCVIII   28th June 2020

'Billions to get Britain Booming' – Mail on Sunday

Everyone cheats a little; stands a bit
too close or doesn't wash for long enough
or can't be bothered not to touch
the merchandise. Look, sometimes we forget;
we shake a hand or pat a back or let
a lover in. The moral tension slips,
the lines grow faint; an accidental kiss
might not be accidental; nights we sweat
our misdemeanours through our dreams,
reporting on the neighbours' barbecues
and broken bubbles. Yes! They're worse
than us, super-spreaders, justly accused.
Now everyone's become the thought police
and everyone's a sinner: confess, confess, confess.

Sonnet XCVIX   29th June 2020

'Hairdressers will be opening on 4th July' – BBC News
After 'Only hair-dryers in Paris ... 1944' by Lee Miller

Well, it's a job. The topless teams of boys
on bicycles are sweating in the vaults
of *Salon Gervais*. Powering the only dryers
in the land, our heroes clad in teeny shorts
display their lovely quadriceps and pedal
onwards. Paris is free: now to the hair.
Coiffure à la mode! Libération! Morale!

Paris, where is our *esprit de la guerre*?

We hunt the beast: part human, part parasite.
Intangible, confused, it's hard to spot.
We power on and try to make some heat.
Meanwhile, corona-cuts: some grow, some buzz,
some cover up. The old freedom is not
an option, evil is not what it was.

Sonnet C   30th June 2020

'Covid-19 death toll passes 500,000 worldwide' – BBC News

'Cannibal rats are among the grimmest consequences of
the upending of urban life' – The Guardian

'Just because it's over doesn't mean it's really over' – Katy Perry

My loves, this is my last. I tip my hat,
I scrawl a wild hurrah, I lightly trip
into the red beyond. Stiff upper lip,
relief, day of the dirt, day of the rats
who eat their own. The rising numbers crack
their own facade, the sonnet slowly sips
its morning tea and speaks: *Let's call it quits.*
To hell with poetry. Bring on the maniacs!
There will be greater griefs. The leading man
is muck and splutter and he has no plan,
the virus finds its host, the wars go on,
the markets rise and fall, the earth is spent.
I hold the sonnet close: my faithful friend,
and hear it sigh. *Damn,* it says, *we are not done.*

Acknowledgements and Thanks

Thanks to the following publications where some of these sonnets appeared, often in different versions:

> *Write Where We Are Now* – Manchester Metropolitan University, *New Boots and Pantisocracies, Field Notes for Survival* - Bad Betty Press, *Her Inside: Women in Lockdown, Anthropocene, And Other Poems,* Barnsley Arts Museum and Archives *#PoetinLockdown* project.

A huge and emotional vote of thanks to my readers and audience on social media who read some of these sonnets hot off the press, shared them and cheered me on.

A big smoochy thank-you to Anja Konig and Miriam Nash, two of my favourite poets, who were with me all the way, every tortuous, exhilarating day of it. Thanks as ever to Norbert Hirschhorn for critique and encouragement, to Robin for a vital close reading, to Uncle Robbie for useful suggestions and daily whooping, to Tamar Yoseloff for commenting on the hefty manuscript, to Sophie Herxheimer for her immense imagination and perfectly empathic cover design.

Thanks also to Jane Commane for her faith in this project and her creative ideas about how to bring it into the world, to Ian McMillan and the producers at The Verb for inviting me to share the sonnets while the project was still under way, to Carol Ann Duffy at MMU for publishing a few poems very early on.

And finally, immense thanks as ever to my family for their patience and respect for the work, for giving me space when space was hard to come by. I love you all.